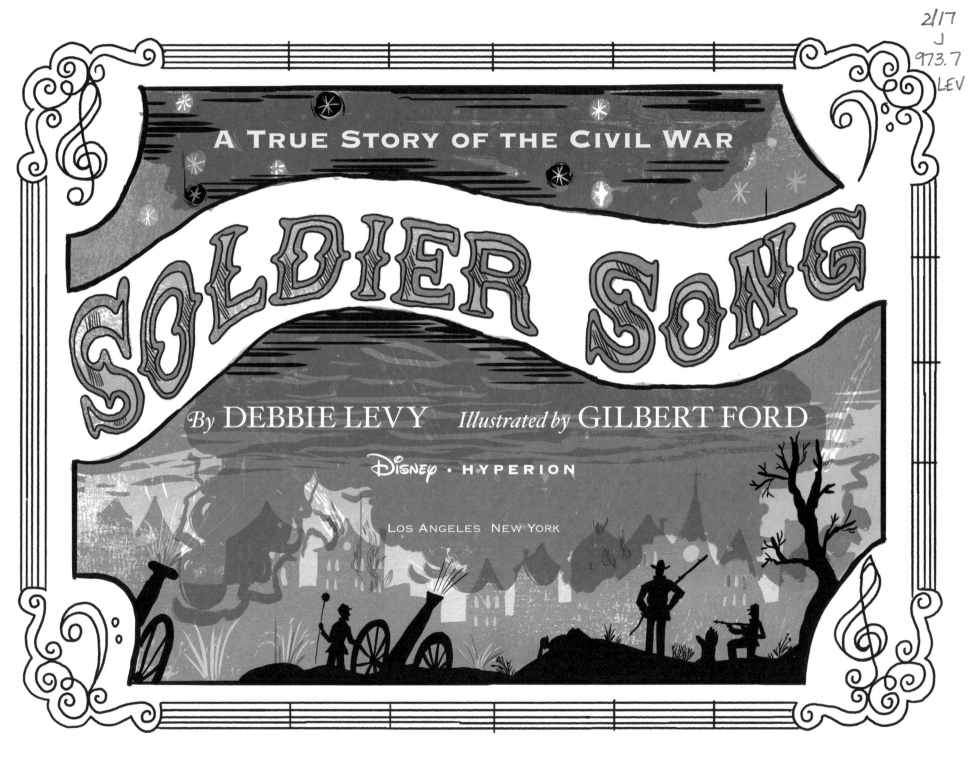

A TRUE STORY OF THE CIVIL WAR

SOLDIER SONG

By DEBBIE LEVY   Illustrated by GILBERT FORD

DISNEY · HYPERION

LOS ANGELES NEW YORK

Union Troops

Confederate Troops

The Union troops used hot air balloons to spy on Confederate troops. The balloons were filled with hydrogen to make them float, but they were very explosive and dangerous to operate.

Thanks to John Hennessy,
Chief Historian/Chief of Interpretation,
Fredericksburg and Spotsylvania National Military Park
for his helpful review and comments.
Any errors are the author's responsibility.

First Edition, February 2017
10 9 8 7 6 5 4 3 2 1
FAC-029191-16288

Printed in Malaysia
Library of Congress Cataloging-in-Publication Data
Names: Levy, Debbie, author. | Ford, Gilbert, illustrator.
Title: Soldier song : a true story of the Civil War / by Debbie Levy ; illustrated by Gilbert Ford.
Description: First edition. | Los Angeles ; New York : Disney Hyperion, 2017.
Identifiers: LCCN 2015019787| ISBN 9781484725986 | ISBN 1484725980
Subjects: LCSH: United States—History--Civil War, 1861-1865—Juvenile literature. |
United States—History—Civil War, 1861-1865—Music and the war—Juvenile literature.
Classification: LCC E468 .L56 2017 | DDC 973.7--dc23
LC record available at http://lccn.loc.gov/2015019787

Reinforced binding
Visit www.DisneyBooks.com

FOR MY FATHER, HAROLD LEVY,
COAST GUARD PHARMACIST'S MATE
IN THE SECOND WORLD WAR, AWARDED THE LEGION OF MERIT
FOR SAVING THE LIVES OF HIS SHIPMATES.
HE ALSO TREATED THE WOUNDED ENEMY.
I THINK HE WOULD HAVE LIKED TO KNOW WHAT HAPPENED
ON THE SHORES OF THE RAPPAHANNOCK RIVER.
—D.L.

FOR MAMAW, WHO ALWAYS ASKS ME
WHEN I'LL BE COMING HOME
—G.F.

DECEMBER 1862

THE CIVIL WAR, America's great and terrible conflict between North and South, was in its second winter. The Southern states had declared themselves the Confederate States of America—a nation they insisted was separate from the "Union" of the United States. In these rebel states, the enslavement of black people would continue to be a way of life. In the Northern states, most people were against slavery— and President Abraham Lincoln called it a "monstrous injustice."

In September 1862, President Lincoln announced the Emancipation Proclamation: "all persons held as slaves" in the rebellious states would be "forever free" as of January 1, 1863. Now, one month before that order was to take effect, the president wanted to back it up with a bold military victory over the rebels. And so, tens of thousands of Union soldiers—called Federals—headed to the Rappahannock River. Their goal was to capture Fredericksburg, Virginia, which lay on the opposite shore . . . and which was held by tens of thousands of Confederate soldiers.

Bugles sounded the order: *Forward!*

The Union soldiers obeyed. They crossed the river on sturdy floating bridges they had built just hours before.

Yankee doodle, keep it up, Yankee doodle dandy! Union bands played this and other jaunty tunes to inspire their soldiers as they marched to the other shore.

The Confederates were ready.

Musket shots split the air. Cannons roared and snorted smoke like dragons. Fiery shells screamed and exploded.

For three fearsome days, the armies fought for control of Fredericksburg.

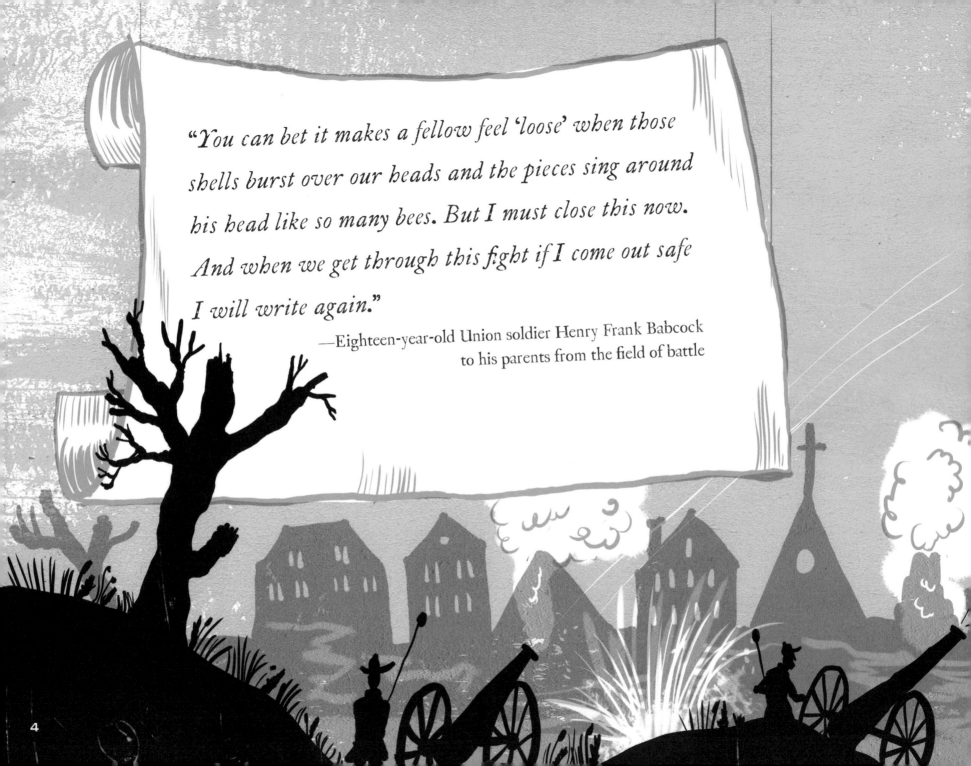

"*You can bet it makes a fellow feel 'loose' when those shells burst over our heads and the pieces sing around his head like so many bees. But I must close this now. And when we get through this fight if I come out safe I will write again.*"

—Eighteen-year-old Union soldier Henry Frank Babcock
to his parents from the field of battle

4

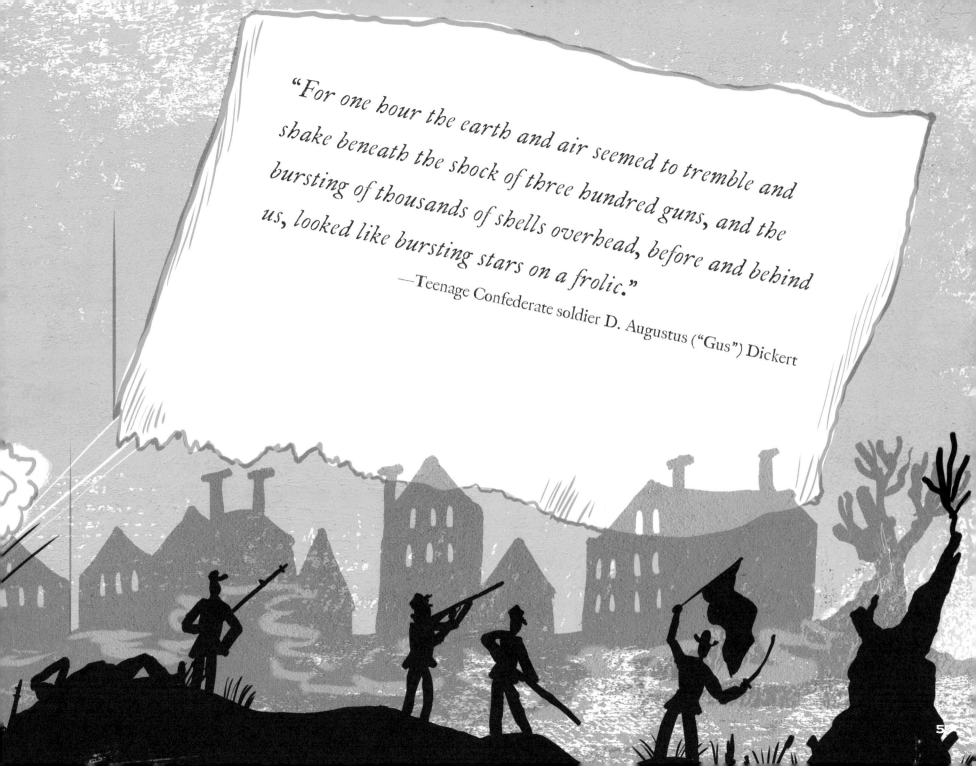

"For one hour the earth and air seemed to tremble and shake beneath the shock of three hundred guns, and the bursting of thousands of shells overhead, before and behind us, looked like bursting stars on a frolic."

—Teenage Confederate soldier D. Augustus ("Gus") Dickert

At first, the Federals seemed to have the advantage. Their exploding shells and lead balls cut down thousands of Confederates.

But the Confederates held the higher ground. Federal soldiers who tried to advance became easy targets. Wave after wave of Northern men and boys fell under a flaming curtain of Southern gunfire.

The din and flame of fighting died down. As thousands lay killed or wounded in freezing fields and muddy hills, fire of a different sort appeared in the sky. This was not the blaze of weapons. This fire was nature's doing.

It was the glow of the aurora borealis—also known as the "northern lights."

"It was very cold and very clear, and the aurora borealis . . . surpassed in splendor any like exhibition I ever saw. Of course we enthusiastic young fellows felt that the heavens were hanging out banners and streamers and setting off fireworks in honor of our victory."

—Confederate soldier Robert Stiles

For the Northern soldiers, the northern lights did not signal victory. The Union army was shredded.

The next day, they prepared to pull back. To prevent the sounds of their retreat from reaching the Confederates, the Federals spread straw on the bridges. They arranged canteens and tin cups in their packs so they wouldn't rattle.

Night fell. A cold rainstorm blew in, and the army of the North quietly stole back across the Rappahannock.

No lively music announced this river crossing.

13

The battle was over. Nothing had been gained. The Federals had begun on the north side of the river—and returned there. The Confederates were still on the south bank of the river, in charge of the city.

On both sides, injured soldiers lay in makeshift hospitals.

Those who weren't injured set up camp. On cold nights, they felt the frozen ground beneath their bedrolls. On warmer days, they wallowed in mud as the earth thawed underfoot.

The two armies—thousands and thousands and thousands of soldiers—dug in for the winter across the ribbon of water from each other.

Neither side was leaving.

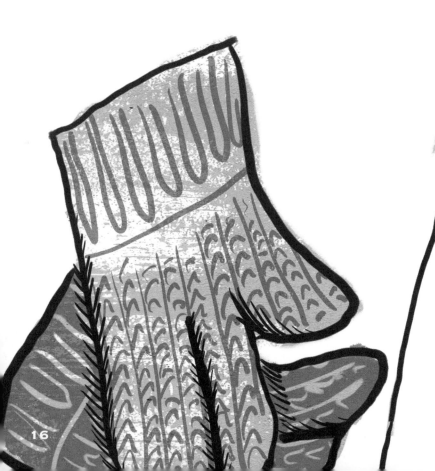

"Dear Friends, Our sufferings have been intense. . . . The ground is hard frozen up; and our poor fellows have nothing but flimsy 'shelter tents,' under which to lie and shiver. Talk about Valley Forge, and the huts Washington and his army had there! Why, they were infinitely better off than we are."
—Union soldier James Rusling

Buglers, fife players, and drummer boys kept the camps on schedule all day long. When soldiers heard the musicians' songs, they knew what they were supposed to do.

"Reveille" was the bugle blare that meant *Wake up!*

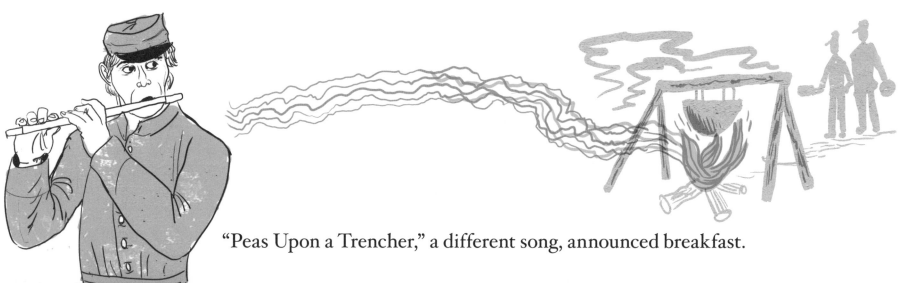

"Peas Upon a Trencher," a different song, announced breakfast.

Another tune, "Surgeon's Call," was the signal for those feeling sick to come to the hospital.

"Fatigue Call" directed soldiers to clean up or get busy with other work around camp.

"Roast Beef" was the nickname for the call to dinner—which certainly was not roast beef.

Whether Billy Yank or Johnny Reb, the soldiers heard the same bugle calls, fife melodies, and drumbeats. After all, just the year before, they had all been part of one, united country, where musicians learned the same tunes.

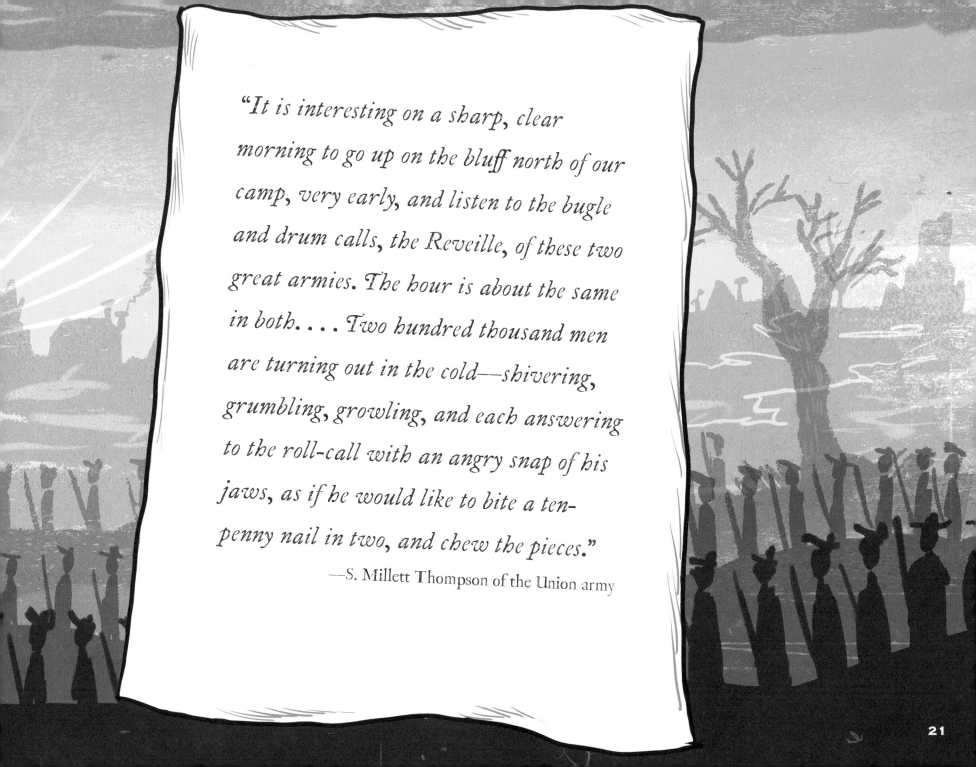

"It is interesting on a sharp, clear morning to go up on the bluff north of our camp, very early, and listen to the bugle and drum calls, the Reveille, of these two great armies. The hour is about the same in both. . . . Two hundred thousand men are turning out in the cold—shivering, grumbling, growling, and each answering to the roll-call with an angry snap of his jaws, as if he would like to bite a ten-penny nail in two, and chew the pieces."

—S. Millett Thompson of the Union army

The soldiers knew they were lucky to have survived the battle. But the Federals were frustrated by their defeat. The Confederates were furious because the town of Fredericksburg was smashed to pieces.

Both Federals and Confederates mourned their friends, killed by the enemy across the river. As Christmas drew near, they all missed their families.

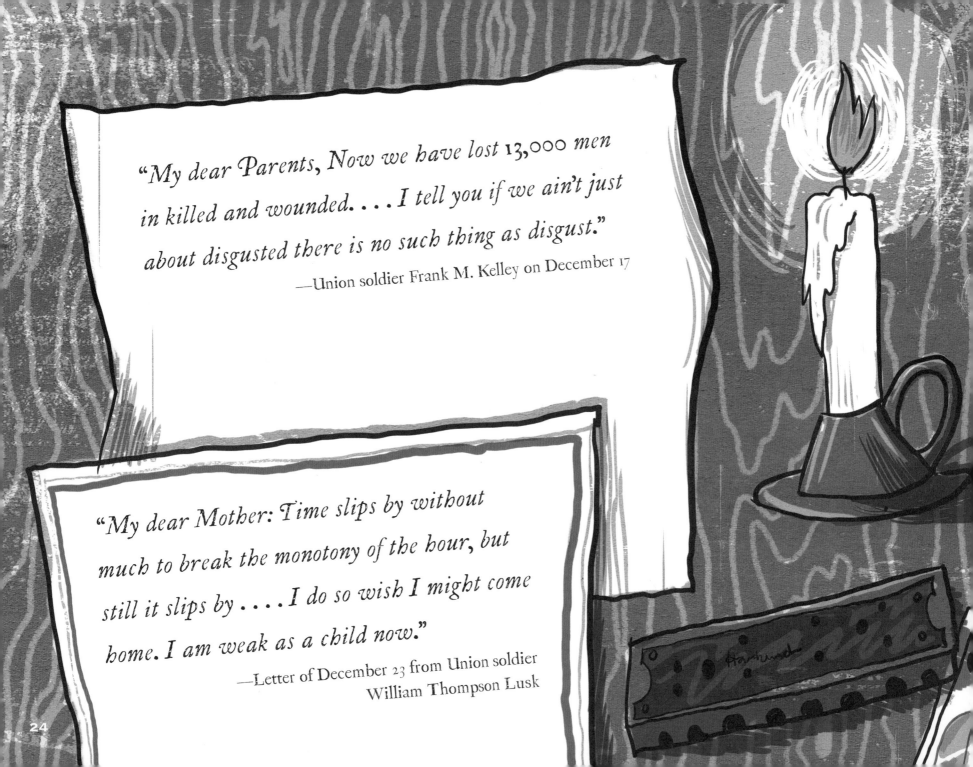

"My dear Parents, Now we have lost 13,000 men in killed and wounded. . . . I tell you if we ain't just about disgusted there is no such thing as disgust."

—Union soldier Frank M. Kelley on December 17

"My dear Mother: Time slips by without much to break the monotony of the hour, but still it slips by . . . . I do so wish I might come home. I am weak as a child now."

—Letter of December 23 from Union soldier
William Thompson Lusk

"The Yankee scoundrels almost completely destroyed Fredericksburg. There ain't much preparation for Christmas in camp."

—Isaac Howard, a teenage Confederate, in a letter of December 25 to his father back in Texas

"My Dearest Wife . . . . Alas! Will the good old times ever return again? And you and I with our little ones dwell together in peace? I hope so. I believe so, but the heart sickens with the deferred hope."

—Letter of December 25 from Confederate soldier P. H. Powers

When they weren't busy with drills or camp work or guard duty, the soldiers passed the time as best they could.

They spent hours writing letters home. They whittled wood and told tall tales.

They wrestled and ran footraces and roasted onions and chased varmints.

And they made music.

The Union forever,
Hurrah! boys, hurrah!
Down with the traitors,
Up with the stars;
While we rally round the flag, boys,
Rally once again,
Shouting the battle cry of Freedom.

—"The Battle Cry of Freedom," a popular Union song

Rebels before, our fathers of yore.
Rebel's the righteous name Washington bore.
Why, then, be ours the same, the name
    that he snatched from shame,
Making it first in fame, foremost in war.
Making it first in fame, foremost in war.

—"God Save the South," a popular Confederate song

Across the river the melodies floated. Sometimes
the soldiers fired tunes back and forth, like musical
cannonballs. Southerners sang their words.

Northerners answered with
different words for the same song.

I wish I was in the land of cot-ton, Old times there are not for-got-ten; Look a-

way! Look a-way! Look a-way! Dix-ie Land. In Dix-ie Land where I was born in, ear-ly on a

fros-ty mor-nin', Look a-way! Look a-way! Look a-way! Dix-ie Land. Then I wish I was in

Dix-ie, Hoo-ray! Hoo-ray! In Dix-ie Land I'll take my stand to live and die in Dix-ie, A-

way, a-way, a-way down south in Dix-ie! A-way, a-way, a-way down south in Dix-ie!

—"Dixie" as sung by Confederate soldiers

A-way down South in the land of trai-tors, Rat-tle snakes and al-li-ga-tors Right a-

way, Come a-way right a-way, Come a-way. Where Cot-ton's King and men are chat-tels, Un-ion boys will

win the bat-tles Right a-way, Come a-way, right a-way, Come a-way, Then we'll all go down to

Dix-ie! A-way! A-way! Each Di-xie boy must un-der-stand that he must mind his un-cle Sam. A-

way! A-way! And we'll all go down to Di-xie! A-way! A-way! And we'll all go down to Di-xie!

—"Dixie" as sung by Union soldiers

Besides the singing, the music of brass bands also soared across the water. The buzz of cornets pierced the air. Velvety notes from deep-throated horns spread like soft blankets. The rattle of side drums kept time.

Bands played at drills and dress parades. They performed for visiting dignitaries.

But to the men and boys camped along the Rappahannock, the bands' most important job was serenading soldiers at day's end.

One afternoon before sundown, the bands struck up their music as usual.

And, also as usual, the concerts turned into a battle of the bands.

The Union bands played tunes dear to a Northerner's heart.

The Confederate bands responded with songs that gladdened a Southerner's soul.

38

The Union soldiers cheered

48

In Dix-ie Land I'll take my stand to live and die in Dix-ie.

The Confederate soldiers yelled their approval.

"The Battle Hymn of the Republic," from the North.

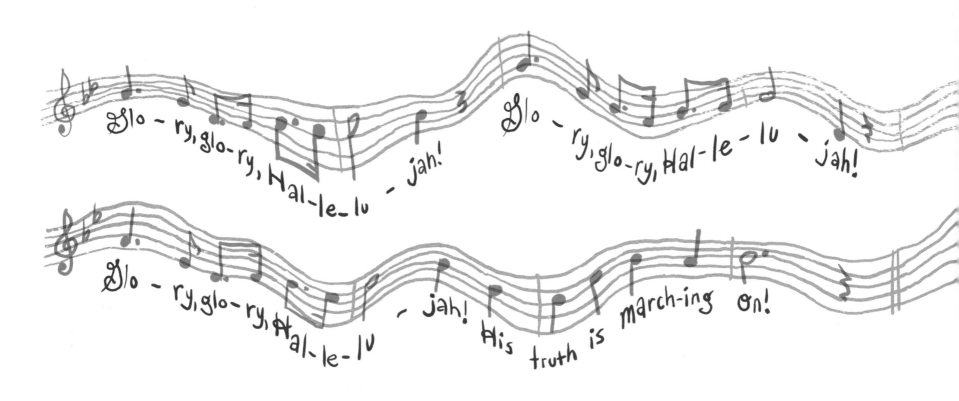

"The Bonnie Blue Flag," from the South.

These were stirring songs of patriotism, loyalty, and courage. These songs made soldiers proud of their side. The songs told the men that their side was right, and the other side wrong.

These were songs for soldiers.

What would be next?

Gentle and slow, the beginning strains of another tune rose over the river.

"Home, Sweet Home." It was a popular song, loved by the entire nation,
North and South. Everyone, everywhere knew "Home, Sweet Home."
From across the river came an answering verse.

It was the other side—the enemy—joining in.

Together, the opposing musicians played the tender melody.
The river was united in song. Everyone knew the words. But
everyone was quiet, listening. Soldiers held the words in their hearts.

"HOME! HOME! SWEET, SWEET HOME! THERE'S NO

This was a song that reminded men of the people and places they had left behind. It reminded them of all they hoped to see again. This, too, was a song for soldiers.

PLACE LIKE HOME; THERE'S NO PLACE LIKE HOME!"

"There was not a sound from anywhere until the tune was finished, and it then seemed as if everybody had gone crazy. I never saw anything to compare with it. Both sides were cheering, jumping up and throwing up hats and doing everything which tended to show enthusiasm. This lasted for at least a half hour. I do believe that had we not had the river between us that the two armies would have gone together and settled the war right there and then."

—Confederate soldier Frank Mixson, who had his sixteenth birthday one week before the battle at Fredericksburg

The cheering died down.

Evening set in. The soldiers ate their smoky, greasy suppers. As darkness deepened, the two armies readied for another winter night.

In the morning, they would again look across the river and see the enemy.

But everyone who heard the song and who heard the cheering knew this. The enemy was also a son, a brother, a husband, a sweetheart. All suffered the same cold and muck, bad food and sickness. All longed for an end to the fighting. And all wanted to go home—North, South, East, and West.

Winter wore on. Federals and Confederates remained camped across the Rappahannock from each other. Conditions were muddy and miserable. Upset stomachs, colds, measles, and other ailments afflicted the soldiers. Spirits were low, especially among the Federals.

Commanders responded to the unhappiness with an order. As Union soldier S. Millett Thompson reported in his journal:

"The bands are forbidden to play pathetic or plaintive tunes, such as 'Home, Sweet Home' . . . lest they serve to dispirit, and unnerve our suffering men."

But the song would not, and did not, disappear.

An order could not erase a tune that men could not forget.

"Home, Sweet Home" rose again on the banks of the Rappahannock. In other camps and fields, too, soldiers kept on playing and singing the song. Sometimes commanders tried to ban it, for fear the words and music made their soldiers too homesick.

The song always came back. As long as soldiers were fighting far from their homes, "Home, Sweet Home" was there with them.

It was a song for soldiers.

JUNE 1865

THE CIVIL WAR was over. The Battle of Fredericksburg had been a low point for the Union. As the war ground on, the Union's fortunes improved. Finally, in the spring of 1865, the Confederates surrendered.

In June, a group of young men who had fought for the South were making their way back home. Their journey took them on a riverboat bound for St. Louis, Missouri. On board the boat were also plenty of Northerners—"too numerous to be comfortable," wrote Philip Stephenson, who had been in the Confederate army during the war.

One night, the teenage Stephenson and his fellow Confederates started singing. As Stephenson later wrote:

"Quickly a crowd gathered around us and grew larger. . . . They knew well enough who we were, but a chord had been struck which vibrated in all hearts, and knew no North, no South. There we were, Rebs serenading Yankees. They kept us singing far into the night and when we wound up with 'Home Sweet Home' the ice was broken completely, and we were on terms of easiest fellowship for the rest of the trip. What creatures we are! What bundles of contradictions!"

THE CIVIL WAR AND THE BATTLE OF FREDERICKSBURG

The Civil War lasted from 1861 to 1865. The Southern states left the Union shortly after the election of President Abraham Lincoln in November 1860. They wanted to preserve the enslavement of black people in their own states, and they wanted slavery allowed in new states that joined the nation. In their view, Southern states had the right to create a new and separate nation if they disagreed with the United States government—and they strongly disagreed with the government of President Lincoln.

President Lincoln was opposed to slavery. He and the Northern states were against allowing slavery to spread to any new states. (When Lincoln became president, there were thirty-four states in total, and seven territories that could one day become states.) The North denied that the South could simply dissolve the Union. These were the central clashes that led to the war, which broke out on April 12, 1861.

Most people, North and South, thought the war would be brief, and thought that their side would win. The Union had a larger army and greater resources. But these advantages did not produce easy victories. By 1862, the North had not dealt the South the types of decisive defeats that could end the war quickly.

The Union did have an important victory in Maryland, at the Battle of Antietam. After that fight, in September 1862, President Lincoln announced the Preliminary Emancipation Proclamation. This order said that on January 1, 1863, slaves in the Confederate states "shall be then, thenceforward, and forever free." President Lincoln wanted to follow up Antietam, and the proclamation, with a big battlefield success. The first chance to do this was at Fredericksburg, Virginia, only fifty miles southwest of Washington, D.C., the Union's capital.

The Battle of Fredericksburg began on December 11, 1862, when the Union army crossed the Rappahannock River. The Federals made their way into the city. But when they tried to advance farther, they were faced with what many later called "a sheet of flame" from the Southern guns. Confederate soldiers were spread out in the hills.

The Union soldiers had no place to hide. On December 13, they were cut down by the thousands in a dreadful, bloody slaughter. The battered Union army retreated back across the river on December 15, and the fight was over.

More soldiers gathered at Fredericksburg to do battle than in any other Civil War battle—more even than in the famous Battle of Gettysburg. The Union army at Fredericksburg, called the Army of the Potomac, fielded approximately 120,000 soldiers. Many former slaves, not yet admitted into Northern armies, also contributed to the Union effort at Fredericksburg as camp attendants, drivers, and in other non-combat roles. The Confederate army, the Army of Northern Virginia, was 78,000 strong. The soldiers on the Union side came from eighteen states. On the Confederate side, soldiers came from twelve states.

Approximately 12,600 Union soldiers were killed or wounded at Fredericksburg. The Confederates suffered 5,300 killed or injured.

After the battle, the Union army set up winter camp on the northern bank of the Rappahannock. The Confederates made camp in Fredericksburg, on the southern bank. (During the Civil War, armies usually stopped fighting and went into camp during the winter months because of weather.) In the hilly terrain, sounds carried easily from one side of the river to another. And since music and military bands were such important parts of army life for North and South during the Civil War, there were plenty of opportunities for "Billy Yank," as the Union soldiers were known, and "Johnny Reb," the nickname for Confederates, to hear each other's songs.

Eyewitness accounts differ on when exactly the emotional rendition of "Home, Sweet Home" on the Rappahannock occurred. Was it right after the battle? At least one soldier's memoir suggests so. (That is Frank Mixson from South Carolina, a teenager at the time of the battle.) Was it on Christmas Eve, a week later? (So wrote John Goolrick, a Fredericksburg resident.) Union soldiers who were there, such as St. Clair Mulholland of

Pennsylvania and Nelson Miles of Massachusetts, placed the concert later. Which side played the very first notes? Different soldiers who were there offer different answers. Mixson wrote that the bands began playing the song at the same time. Mulholland of Pennsylvania, as well as a Mississippi soldier, both stated that the Federals first struck up the song, and the Confederates followed.

Those who survived the Battle of Fredericksburg witnessed frightful scenes of chaos and death. It is not really surprising that, amid these awful experiences, the exact timing of an evening concert has been lost to history. But what is not lost is that a simple song, "Home, Sweet Home," bridged the divide between war's enemies.

NOTABLE PEOPLE AT FREDERICKSBURG

Many notable people participated at or were connected to the Battle of Fredericksburg. Here are some of them:

GENERAL AMBROSE BURNSIDE commanded the Union Army of the Potomac at Fredericksburg. Burnside was well known for the showy whiskers he grew on the sides of his face. He, his whiskers, and his name gave rise to the word "sideburns."

GENERAL ROBERT E. LEE led the Confederate Army of Northern Virginia at Fredericksburg. Before the war, he was an officer in the United States Army. After the South left the Union, President Lincoln offered Lee command of the Union army. Lee, who was from the Southern state of Virginia, joined the Confederate side instead.

The poet WALT WHITMAN traveled to Fredericksburg just after the battle. He went in search of his brother George, who fought for the Union. Whitman found George, only slightly injured, and then spent time in camp, especially with the wounded soldiers. In 1865, Whitman published a book of poems inspired by his Civil War experiences, entitled *Drum-Taps.* Whitman became one of the most famous poets in American literature.

CLARA BARTON volunteered to care for injured soldiers as soon as the Civil War broke out. She traveled with the Union army to many battlefields. During the Battle of Fredericksburg, she tended the wounded in the thick of the fighting in the town. She also worked tirelessly in makeshift hospitals in the Union camp. After the war, Barton founded the American Red Cross, which provides relief and assistance to people in times of disaster and hardship.

LOUISA MAY ALCOTT volunteered at a Washington, D.C., hospital during the winter of 1862–63. She helped care for many of the grievously wounded soldiers who were brought there from the Fredericksburg battlefield. She wrote about this experience in a book published in 1863, called *Hospital Sketches.* Five years later, Alcott wrote *Little Women,* the novel that made her famous.

FRANKLIN THOMPSON, a soldier from Flint, Michigan, carried messages back and forth from Union headquarters to the battle's front lines at Fredericksburg. But Franklin Thompson wasn't this soldier's real name; he was actually a woman, Sarah Emma Edmonds, who disguised herself as a man and served in the Union army until falling ill with malaria in 1863.

ABNER DOUBLEDAY was a Union general at Fredericksburg. Years later, Doubleday became known as the inventor of the game of baseball—even though he had never made such a claim himself and seems never to have mentioned the game in his writings. Still, the Baseball Hall of Fame is located in Doubleday's hometown, Cooperstown, New York, in his honor.

WINSLOW HOMER was a young artist who visited Virginia battlefields during the Civil War as a magazine sketch artist. In 1863, Homer had the first major show of his paintings in New York City. One canvas in particular caught the admiring attention of the public. It was entitled *Home, Sweet Home.* The painting shows two Union soldiers in camp, standing in front of their tent. In the near distance, a band is playing music—presumably the song of the painting's title. This painting marked the beginning of Winslow Homer's career as a painter. He later became one of America's best-known artists.

THE SONG

The words to "Home, Sweet Home" were written by John Howard Payne. Born in New York in 1791, Payne composed the poem that became the song "Home, Sweet Home" for an operetta that was staged in London in 1823. Henry Bishop, a famous English composer of the day, wrote the music. The song immediately became tremendously popular. The song's publisher earned a great deal of money by selling thousands of song sheets. Payne, however, did not share in this wealth. His name wasn't even listed on the sheet music.

Later, Payne did receive recognition for writing "Home, Sweet Home." In Washington, D.C., in 1850, the celebrated singer Jenny Lind gave a concert. President Millard Fillmore and the famous senators Henry Clay and Daniel Webster were in the audience. So was John Howard Payne. Lind loved "Home, Sweet Home." Knowing Payne was in the audience, she turned toward him and sang his song. Many in the audience cried at the moving scene. When Lind finished, Senator Webster rose from his seat and bowed to Payne. The rest of the audience gave Payne a standing ovation. He died two years later at the age of sixty-one.

During the Civil War, at a private concert at the White House, President Abraham Lincoln and his wife, Mary, were mourning the recent death of their twelve-year-old son, Willie. An Italian singer named Adelina Patti could not help but notice that the couple were in tears as she came to the end of her performance. She wanted to sing something that would comfort them, and started on a cheerful tune when the president made a request. Would she sing "Home, Sweet Home"? Patti did not know the words, and did not have a copy of the music. The president did. He retrieved it, handed it over to Patti, and she sang the song.

You can hear historic recordings of "Home, Sweet Home" at these websites:

Library of Congress, National Jukebox, The Haydn Quartet, recorded March 12, 1902. http://www.loc.gov/jukebox/recordings/detail/id/7635/

Library of Congress, National Jukebox, Richard Jose, recorded February 23, 1906. http://www.loc.gov/jukebox/recordings/detail/id/975/

You can listen to other music mentioned in this book at these websites:

Bugle calls, U.S. Army Music website, http://www.music.army.mil/music/buglecalls/default.asp

"The Battle Cry of Freedom," Library of Congress, National Jukebox, Raymond Dixon, recorded February 18, 1914. http://www.loc.gov/jukebox/recordings/detail/id/3748

"God Save the South," National Anthems website, http://www.nationalanthems.info/csa.htm

"Dixie," Library of Congress, National Jukebox, Victor Military Band, recorded February 5, 1914. http://www.loc.gov/jukebox/recordings/detail/id/6390

"Yankee Doodle," Library of Congress, National Jukebox, Victor Military Band, recorded January 19, 1914. http://www.loc.gov/jukebox/recordings/detail/id/3696

"The Battle Hymn of the Republic," Library of Congress, National Jukebox, Reinald Werrenrath, recorded July 12, 1917. http://www.loc.gov/jukebox/recordings/detail/id/5493

"The Bonnie Blue Flag," recorded by Elizabeth Knight and The Harvesters, The Kennedy Center ArtsEdge, *When Music Goes Marching to War,* http://artsedge.kennedy-center.org/educators/how-to/american-history-and-music/teaching-civil-war-music.aspx#on-the-home-front

TIME LINE OF THE CIVIL WAR

November 1860 — Abraham Lincoln is elected sixteenth president of the United States.

December 1860 — South Carolina secedes (separates) from the Union.

January–February 1861 — Alabama, Florida, Georgia, Louisiana, Mississippi, and Texas secede from the Union. The secessionist states begin forming the Confederate States of America and choose as president Jefferson Davis, who was once a U.S. senator and secretary of war under President Franklin Pierce.

March 1861 — Lincoln is inaugurated as president.

April 1861 — Confederate forces fire on Fort Sumter in Charleston Harbor, South Carolina. This is the beginning of the Civil War.

April–June 1861 — Arkansas, North Carolina, Virginia, and Tennessee secede from the Union. Richmond, Virginia becomes the capital of the Confederacy. . . .

July 1861 — The Confederates defeat the Union at the First Battle of Bull Run in Manassas, Virginia.

March 1862 — Military history is made when the first battle between ironclad, rather than wooden, warships takes place between the Union *Monitor* and the Confederate *Merrimac,* in the harbor at Hampton Roads, Virginia. Neither side is a clear winner, but the era of wooden warships is over.

April 1862 — The Union wins the Battle of Shiloh, Tennessee, and also forces the surrender of New Orleans, Louisiana.

May–June 1862 — Confederates succeed in driving Union forces out of Virginia's Shenandoah Valley in the Shenandoah Campaign.

June–July 1862 — The Union tries to take over the Confederate capital of Richmond in the Seven Days Battles, but fails.

August 1862 — The Confederates again defeat the Union in Manassas, Virginia, at the Second Battle of Bull Run.

September 1862 — In Sharpsburg, Maryland, the Union beats back a Confederate drive into the North at the Battle of Antietam. Shortly after, President Lincoln announces the Preliminary Emancipation Proclamation, which states that all enslaved people in the Confederacy will be free as of January 1, 1863.

December 1862 — The Confederates defeat the Union at the Battle of Fredericksburg.

January 1863	The Emancipation Proclamation becomes effective. It specifically invites newly freed men to join the Union armed forces.
May 1863	The Confederates win the Battle of Chancellorsville, Virginia.
July 1863	The Union defeats the Confederates at the Battle of Gettysburg, Pennsylvania. The three-day fight results in more killed and wounded than in any other battle in the war. The battle marks the end of the Confederacy's attempt to invade the North. The day after the Battle of Gettysburg, on July 4, the Confederates surrender Vicksburg, Mississippi, to the Union.
November 1863	At a gathering to dedicate the soldiers' cemetery at Gettysburg, President Lincoln gives the Gettysburg Address. Beginning with the words "Four score and seven years ago our fathers brought forth on this continent a new nation," this brief speech is one of the most famous texts in American history.
June 1864	The Union begins the siege of Petersburg, Virginia, which lasts almost until the end of the war.
September 1864	The Union takes over Atlanta, Georgia.
November 1864	President Lincoln is reelected. Union General William T. Sherman and soldiers march from Atlanta to Savannah, Georgia. The march becomes infamous for the severe property destruction inflicted by Union soldiers along their route.
December 1864	The Union takes over Savannah, Georgia.
March 1865	President Lincoln is inaugurated for a second term of office.
April 1865	On April 3, the Union takes over Richmond, the capital of Virginia, and Petersburg. On April 9, General Robert E. Lee surrenders the Confederate Army of the Potomac to Union General Ulysses S. Grant at Appomattox Court House, Virginia. Although other Confederate forces will surrender in other places during April and May, Appomattox marks the end of the Civil War.
	On April 14, John Wilkes Booth assassinates President Lincoln in Washington, D.C. Lincoln's vice president, Andrew Johnson, becomes the seventeenth president of the United States.
May 1865	Union soldiers capture Jefferson Davis, the president of the Confederacy, in Georgia. Davis is imprisoned for two years and then released in 1867.

Selected Bibliography

Primary sources

These are firsthand accounts of events that happened at the Battle of Fredericksburg and elsewhere in the Civil War. Many of the old books are freely available on the internet.

Army of the Potomac, History of Its Campaign, The Peninsula, Maryland, Fredericksburg, Testimony of Its Three Commanders Before the Congressional Committee on the Conduct of the War. New York: Tribune Association, 1863.

Henry Frank Babcock, letter to his parents, December 14, 1862. (Online at *Civil War Voices* website, http://www.soldierstudies.org /blog/2010/06/battle-of-fredericksburg-letter/)

Leander W. Cogswell, *A History of the Eleventh New Hampshire Regiment, Volunteer Infantry in the Rebellion War, 1861–1865.* Concord, New Hampshire: Republican Press Association, 1891.

Charles William Bardeen, *A Little Fifer's War Diary.* Syracuse, New York: C.W. Bardeen, Publisher, 1910.

Eugene A. Cory, *A Private's Recollections of Fredericksburg.* Providence, Rhode Island: Rhode Island Soldiers and Sailors Historical Society, 1884.

Orson Blair Curtis, *History of the Twenty-Fourth Michigan of the Iron Brigade.* Detroit, Michigan: Winn & Hammond, 1891.

D. Augustus Dickert, *History of Kershaw's Brigade, with Complete Roll of Companies, Biographical Sketches, Incidents, Anecdotes, Etc.* Newberry, South Carolina: Elbert H. Aull Company, 1899.

John Dwyer, *Address of John Dwyer, Hudson Falls, N. Y., Major 63d N. Y. V., Senior Officer Living of the Irish Brigade Association,* December 12, 1914. New York: Herald Press, 1915.

Joseph F. Green, letter to Juliana Reynolds from camp near Falmouth, Virginia, January 2, 1863. (Online at http://www.loc.gov/resource /mreynolds.008001)

David E. Johnston, *The Story of a Confederate Boy in the Civil War.* Portland, Oregon: Glass & Prudhomme Company, 1914.

Frank M. Kelley, letter to his parents, headed "General Griffin's Hd. Qrs. Camp near Fredericksburg, Va.," December 17, 1862. (Online at *Museum Quality Americana* website, http://www.mqamericana.com/44th_ NY_Fredericksburg.html)

Oscar Lapham, *Recollections of Service in the Twelfth Regiment, R.I. Volunteers.* Providence, Rhode Island: Rhode Island Soldiers and Sailors Historical Society, 1885.

William Thompson Lusk, *War Letters of William Thompson Lusk.* New York: 1911, privately printed.

Charles S. McClenthen, *Narrative of the Fall & Winter Campaign, by a Private Soldier.* Syracuse, New York: Masters & Lee Book and Job Printers, 1863.

Nelson A. Miles, *Serving the Republic: Memoirs of the Civil and Military Life of Nelson A. Miles, Lieutenant-General, United States Army.* New York: Harper & Brothers, 1911.

Frank M. Mixson, *Reminiscences of a Private, Company "E" 1st S. C. Vols. (Hagood's).* Columbia, South Carolina: The State Company, 1910.

St. Clair A. Mulholland, *The Story of the 116th Regiment Pennsylvania Volunteers in the War of the Rebellion.* Philadelphia: F. McManus, Jr. & Co., 1903.

P. H. Powers, letter to his wife, December 25, 1862. (Online at University of Virginia Library, http://vshadow.vcdh.virginia.edu/head/A0321)

James Fowler Rusling, *Men and Things I Saw in Civil War Days.* New York: Eaton & Mains Press, 1899.

Philip Daingerfield Stephenson, *The Civil War Memoir of Philip Daingerfield Stephenson*, edited by Nathaniel Cheairs Hughes, Jr. Baton Rouge, Louisiana: Louisiana State University Press, 1998.

Robert Stiles, *Four Years Under Marse Robert*. New York and Washington: The Neale Publishing Company, 1904.

S. Millett Thompson, *Thirteenth Regiment of New Hampshire Volunteer Infantry in the War of the Rebellion, 1861–1865, A Diary Covering Three Years and a Day*. Boston: Houghton, Mifflin and Company, 1888.

University of North Carolina at Chapel Hill Library, *The Civil War Day by Day*. (Letters and other documents.) (Online at http://blogs.lib.unc.edu/civilwar/)

Secondary sources

Bruce Catton, *The Civil War*. Boston: Houghton Mifflin, 2005.

Center of Military History, United States Army, *Fredericksburg Staff Ride Briefing Book*. U.S. Government Printing Office, 2004-304-138/95484.

Civil War Trust website. www.civilwar.org

Shelby Foote, *The Civil War: A Narrative: Fredericksburg to Meridian*. New York: Random House, 1963.

Fredericksburg & Spotsylvania National Military Park website. www.nps.gov/frsp/

John T. Goolrick, *Historic Fredericksburg: The Story of an Old Town*. Richmond, Virginia: Whittet & Shepperson, 1922.

Eleanor Jones Harvey, *The Civil War and American Art*. New Haven: Yale University Press, 2012.

Winslow Homer, *Home, Sweet Home* (oil painting). National Gallery of Art website. http://www.nga.gov/feature/homer/homer03.htm

Helen Kendrick Johnson, *Our Familiar Songs and Those Who Made Them*. New York: Henry Holt and Company, 1909.

Lincoln Home National Historic Site website. www.nps.gov/liho

James M. McPherson, *Battle Cry of Freedom: The Civil War Era*. New York: Oxford University Press, 1988.

National Park Service Civil War Series: The Battle of Fredericksburg, 2007. (Online at www.nps.gov/parkhistory/online_books/civil_war_series/15/)

Francis Augustin O'Reilly, *The Fredericksburg Campaign: Winter War on the Rappahannock*. Baton Rouge, Louisiana: Louisiana State University Press, 2006.

George C. Rable, *Fredericksburg! Fredericksburg!* Chapel Hill: University of North Carolina Press, 2002.

Further reading for young people

Joy Hakim, *War, Terrible War*. New York: Oxford University Press, 2003.

Sid Hite, *The Journal of Rufus Rowe*. New York: Scholastic, 2003. (Historical fiction.)

K. M. Kostyal, *1862, Fredericksburg: A New Look at a Bitter Civil War Battle*. Washington, D.C.: National Geographic Children's Books, 2011.

James M. McPherson, *Fields of Fury: The American Civil War*. New York: Atheneum Books for Young Readers, 2002.

Jim Murphy, *The Boys' War: Confederate and Union Soldiers Talk About the Civil War*. New York: Clarion Books, 1990.

Delia Ray, *Behind the Blue and Gray: The Soldier's Life in the Civil War*. New York: Dutton, 1991.

QUOTATION SOURCES

"Monstrous injustice." Speech at Peoria, Illinois, October 16, 1854. Lincoln Home National Historic Site website.

"Forever free." Preliminary Emancipation Proclamation, September 22, 1862. National Archives website. http://www.archives.gov

"You can bet." Letter from Henry Frank Babcock, December 14, 1862. Babcock came from New York.

"For one hour." D. Augustus Dickert, *History of Kershaw's Brigade*, page 183. Dickert came from South Carolina.

"It was very cold." Robert Stiles, *Four Years Under Marse Robert*, page 137. Stiles came from New York but left the North to fight for the Confederates.

"Dear Friends." Letter dated December 21, 1862, James Fowler Rusling, *Men and Things I Saw in Civil War Days*, pages 290–91. Rusling came from New Jersey.

"It is interesting." S. Millett Thompson, *Thirteenth Regiment of New Hampshire Volunteer Infantry in the War of the Rebellion*, page 105. Thompson came from New Hampshire.

"My dear Parents." Letter from Frank M. Kelley, December 17, 1862. Kelley came from New York.

"My dear Mother." Letter of December 23, 1862, William Thompson Lusk, *War Letters of William Thompson Lusk*, pages 257–58. Lusk came from Connecticut.

"The Yankee scoundrels." Letter from Isaac Adams Howard to his father, December 25, 1862, from University of North Carolina Library, *The Civil War Day by Day*. Howard came from Texas.

"My Dearest Wife." Letter from P. H. Powers, December 25, 1862. Powers came from Virginia.

"The Union forever." Words to "The Battle Cry of Freedom" are from "Civil War Music: Battle Cry of Freedom," Civil War Trust website.

"Rebels before, our fathers of yore." Words to "God Save the South" are from "Civil War Music: God Save the South," Civil War Trust website.

"Dixie." Words to the Southern and Northern versions of "Dixie" are from the Civil War Trust website.

"Yankee Doodle." Words to "Yankee Doodle" are from Library of Congress, Performing Arts Encyclopedia. http://lcweb2.loc.gov/diglib/ihas/loc.natlib.ihas.100010484/default.html

"Glory, glory." Words to "The Battle Hymn of the Republic" are from "Civil War Music: The Battle Hymn of the Republic," Civil War Trust website.

"Hurrah! Hurrah!" Words to "The Bonnie Blue Flag" are from "Civil War Music: Bonnie Blue Flag," Civil War Trust website.

"'Mid pleasures and palaces." Words to "Home, Sweet Home" are from Helen Kendrick Johnson, *Our Familiar Songs*, page 44.

"There was not a sound." Frank M. Mixson, *Reminiscences of a Private*, pages 37–38. Mixson came from South Carolina.

"The bands are forbidden." S. Millett Thompson, *Thirteenth Regiment*, page 104.

"Quickly a crowd gathered." Philip Daingerfield Stephenson, *The Civil War Memoir of Philip Daingerfield Stephenson*, page 381. Stephenson came from Missouri and went south to join the Confederate cause when he was fifteen.